Army Barmy
Revised Edition

By

Clive Ward

In memory of Little Eddie, a great friend, sadly missed and all my Army comrades.

It's 18:30 hrs, the 10 of September 1974. It's pissing down with rain. I'm sitting at Derby bus station, waiting for the number 42 bus, to take me to Whittington Barracks, Lichfield. I'd joined the Army, the infantry why? Fucked if I know, it was just something to do, most of my mates had joined up so I did, I was 16 years old.

After serving 2 years as a boy soldier, I was now nearly 18, bullied and beaten into shape, and ready to join my regiment, the Worcestershire and Sherwood Foresters, nicknamed the Woofers, based in Colchester. I went on to serve for another 12 years.

A lot of my memories are all too distant now, but some things you never forget. I've already written a book called, "The Unnamed Soldiers," about all the things I witnessed, and what happened to me, during the 14 years I

spent in the army. Like they say, you can't take them with you, but in that book you definitely can!
So in this book, some of what I've written is true, but mainly it's fiction. What I've tried to do is, recall some of the situations I witnessed, and tied them all up into one funny story.

Hopefully you'll find mostly original content, but you're bound to find a bits and pieces you've heard before in there somewhere.

In my story, I've cut down the amount of characters I've used, it would have been too confusing with everyone I remember, so I've concentrated on a handful, but I think you'll find I've covered every personality.

I hope you enjoy reading it, and it brings back good memories, here goes… oh, sorry about the bad language, but it had to stay in, it wouldn't be right without it.

Also, in case you have a problem understanding all the army slang, you'll find a useful glossary at the back of the book.

Chapter one

I'd been given an army train warrant, which meant I didn't have to pay, but the down side of that is, the army will send you by the cheapest possible route. If that meant stopping at every minor station on the planet, that's what happened. Anybody who served in the forces, during the 1980's, I'm sure, would have gone on one of those magical mystery tours.

It's late in the evening, I'm sitting on the train, on my way to Colchester. I'd missed my connection at the last station, and now my train was running late, god knows what time I'll arrive!! But I'm ok, the army made sure I wouldn't go hungry. Before I left, I was issued with my standard white box, consisting of 1 x apple, 1 boiled egg, "at least a week old, great for clearing train carriages," Sweaty cheese sandwiches, and a packet of 3 biscuits, usually digestive.

My future comrades were sitting on their beds in the **barrack room,** some were preparing their kit for the next day, and some were just chilling out, in other words, they couldn't be arsed, they'd wait till the last minute.

"Look at the shine on those boots, what do you reckon Eddie? I bet you wish you could get your boots that good?" said Doris with a smile on his face, a mile wide, he'd been **bulling** his boots.

Private Graham Day, nick name Doris, a bit of a creep, arse licker, he's so far up the Platoon Commander's arse, his feet don't touch the ground. Every platoon had them, but somehow, they'd nearly always end up with egg on their face.
"What the fuck are you doing that for? You're trying to show us all up, aren't you? Arse creeping bastard," Eddie said.

Private Eddie Edwards the old soldier of the platoon, aged 30, he's been in the army for a good few years, in fact too long, he's not interested in promotion, he's what you call **Non Tac**, he knows how to twist people round his little finger, an expert at shit stirring and winding people up, a good mate to have on your side when the shit hits the fan, and it generally does when Eddie's around.

Doris always had that smug smile on his face, as though he knew better.

"It's called pride Eddie," said Doris. "Something you haven't got, and never will have, you can walk round like a bag of shit, if you want. I've got standards to keep up. I'm going places."

Eddie paused and lowered his **Wank mag,** then sparked up another fag.

 "Well hurry up and fuck off then, and give us all a break will you."
"Why, where are you going Doris?" Wocko asked.

Private Watkinson, nick name Wocko, thicker than a Sperm whale Omelette, a walking germ factory, definitely not first in the queue, when the bars of soap were handed out. Oh well, he's somebody's son, but definitely should have been shot at birth.

"You know what I mean. When I get promoted," said Doris, with that smug look on his face.

Eddie laughed, "Promoted you!? God help us, if you were leading us into battle! You're in dream world Doris. You'll never get a stripe on your arm, as long as you've got a hole in your arse. "

Wocko, picked up his combat trousers, and discovered a rather large hole, in the crotch area.

"Talking about holes, look at this bastard, I don't fucking believe it, it must be those **cook house** beans."

He got up, and walked casually over to Doris's bed space. As Wocko ventured nearer, Doris kicked his locker door shut.

"What do you want Wocko?"
"Eh, Doris, do us a favour, and lend me your needle and cotton, to sew this hole up, there's a pal"
"What did your last servant die of? There's a **NAAFI** down the road. Instead of wasting your money on fags, fruit machines and mars bars, try buying a sewing kit, like I had to, and while you're down there, buy some deodorant."

Wocko looked at his watch.

"But its shut… come on don't be such a tight bastard, aren't you going to help your fellow roommate out, in his hour of need… please! If we were in battle, I'd give you my last bullet, I would."
"Would you WOCKO, said Doris smiling."
"Course I would, you're my mate."

"I would too…." Said Eddie, "In his fucking head… forget it Wocko, you're wasting your time, he wouldn't do anything for anyone, apart from himself.
"That's a lie, I'm always helping Wocko out, in fact, it was only yesterday I gave him a bar of soap."
"That was a bar of soap?" said Wocko, "I wondered why it tasted fucking weird!"

Eddie laughed and carried on reading his wank mag.

"And by the way, you're the last person I'd help Edwards."
"Oh yeah."
"Yes."
"Are you sure about that?"
"Yes."

Eddie jumped off his bed, walked over to Doris, and grabbed his boots, Doris began to panic.

"Eh, watch what you're doing? I spent bloody hours on them, give me them back, they're mine."

Eddie, handed Doris a scruffy pair of boots, in return.

"These are yours, I switched them, when you were down the NAAFI, this afternoon."

They all laughed, Doris was dumb struck, opened mouthed, then he started to go red.

"You wanker! You fucking wanker. You mean I've been bulling your boots, for the last four hours."
"Yep... I was going to say something, but you were doing such a good job."

Eddie pointed to a spot on his new looking, shiny boots.

"Tut, you've missed a bit look! If you're going to do the job, do it properly will you."

Doris looks down at his scruffy boots, he looks like he's about to burst into tears.

"We've got an inspection tomorrow morning... What am I supposed to do now?"

"It looks like you're in shit street, doesn't it Doris. I could loan you mine, but it'll cost you."
 "And I've run out of polish," Doris replied.
"You know what they say Doris, preparation and planning, prevents, piss poor performance..."

Doris looked at Eddie shaking his head in disgust.

"And before you ask, I haven't got any polish, why do you think I got you to do them. It looks like your promotion hopes have taken a bit of a nose dive, creep arse, why don't you ask Wocko, if he's got any polish."

In desperation, Doris turns to Wocko.

"Wocko, mate, I'll do you a trade. Your polish, for my needle and cotton."
"How does fuck off, grab you... there's a NAAFI down the road."

Eddie started to laugh loudly.

"But it's shut. Come on Wocko, please. I'll even sew that hole up for you. Please Wocko."

That was an offer Wocko couldn't refuse.

"Okay, it's a deal, my polish is in my locker... somewhere?"

Wocko hands over his grotty pair of trousers, to Doris, who accepted them reluctantly.

Doris approached Wocko's bed space with caution, and slowly opened Wocko's **locker** door, like he was dealing with a UXB. The fumes hit him instantly, he put his hand over his mouth and nose, the smell was too much and he backed off.

"On second thoughts forget it, I'll give it a miss. I'd need a battalion Of Ghurkhas, to search that rat infested shit hole."
"Will you shut that locker door Wocko, it fucking stinks, my eyes are starting to water," Eddie shouted.

Suddenly, the door burst open, this was when I appeared on the scene, better late than never, the train had broken down and I was late.

My first introduction to my new roommates, was the smell of Wocko's locker. I'll never forget that smell. I walked into the barrack room, accompanied by my new section commander **Cpl** Clark.

Cpl Lee Clark, nick name Corpse, way out of his depth, he might be a corporal, but he couldn't handle the pressure, or his men most of the time, a bit of a loner, worries too much, spends his whole army career, trying to stop Eddie getting the better of him.

There was silence in the room, I struggled with my case and kit bag. Cpl Clark directed me to my new bed space, slap bang between Eddie and Doris, and directly opposite Wocko, a lovely sight to wake up to, first thing in the morning.

"Right Ward, un-pack your gear, lights out in ten minutes, reveille 0630. Shit, shower and shave, breakfast 0700, **room jobs** completed by 0730. Area's done by 0745, on parade 0800... Got that, any questions?"

I looked down at my new bed, minus its mattress.

"Yeah, so what do I sleep on Corporal? There's no mattress."

Cpl Clark started laughing.

"This isn't a fucking holiday camp, try bed springs, if you'd have got here three hours ago, like you were supposed to, you would have had a mattress, the stores were open then. Any more stupid questions?"
"No Corporal."

Cpl Clarke addressed the room.

"This is Private Ward. He's a new member of our Platoon. Make sure he knows the score, for tomorrow morning's inspection."

"Eh Corpse, you couldn't do the honours, and tuck us in down the bottom. There's a terrible draught blowing around my feet," said Eddie. "Shut it you, it's not Corpse, it's Corporal and it's not too late for a run round the **square,** in full kit, and that goes for the rest of you as well."

Corpse started to walk out of the door, when Eddie commented from behind his magazine.

"Gets a couple of stripes, and they go to his fucking head."

Cpl Clark popped his head around the door.

"What was that Edwards, got something to say?"
"Nothing Corpse, I was just telling new boy, he'd better hurry up and get in bed."

Cpl Clarke started to walk towards me stopped, then pointed to Eddie, who was smiling.

"A word of warning Ward, keep away from him, he's trouble. Do you hear me?" Forgetting the fact, I'd just been given a bed about 6 feet away from him!
"Yes, Corporal."
"Lights out in 10 minutes."

Doris started to panic.

"10 minutes... But I haven't finished doing my kit yet."
"Tough shit. You should've thought of that earlier." Said Cpl Clark, before he left the room.

I sat on my bed for a moment, taking it all in, no mattress, Wocko's smell, Doris's moaning and Eddie's cockiness, is this it? Is this what I'd joined the Army for? I was really looking forward to joining my unit, surely things would get better than this. I wanted to make a good impression on my new roommates. Eddie was the first to speak.

"So what do they call you then, new boy?"
"New boy! My mates call me Wardie."
"You're going to have to earn that new boy, from now on, your name's new boy, got that new boy. Got any smokes new boy."

I quickly got my cigarettes out, they were the only thing I had to offer, apart from a boiled egg and sweaty cheese sandwiches, but it didn't take Wocko long, to sniff those out.

"Eh new boy, do you want these sandwiches? Oh, and a boiled egg, bonus."
"No, you can have them."
"I'll have the digestive biscuits, said Eddie."
Now how the fuck did he know I had them, he must have ex-ray vision.

I put my pack of 20 fags, on my bedside locker, it didn't take long before, Doris and Wocko appeared, they all ambushed my fag packet, Eddie took 2.

"Hey, they've, got to last me, till payday."

They, of course ignored me.

"How long have you signed up for, new boy?" Eddie asked.
"12 years."
"12 years? I'll give you 12 weeks."
"What makes you say that?"

"You don't look the type. I'll give you six weeks, and you'll be crying home to Mummy, to buy you out, like the rest of them. We've seen 'em come, and we've seen 'em go. Haven't we lads? And you're a seen 'em go, new boy."

I just ignored Eddie, and let him have his say, I'd sussed him out. I knew it would pay off, to stay on the same side. I started to unpack my gear, into my locker.

"So, how long have you been in?" I asked, looking at Eddie.

Doris and Wocko, started to laugh, Eddie looked surprised by the question.

"I've changed my mind…. Make that six fucking seconds."
"Eddie joined when the Dead Sea was still alive, and Pontius Pilate was flying for Galilee Airways, didn't you Eddie?" Doris said laughing.

Doris started to dig around in my locker. I looked on in disapproval, I'd been here less than half an hour, and they were rooting through my stuff.

"Eh, new boy, you haven't got any black polish, have you?"
"Err, no, sorry mate, I've got to get some."

I carried on unpacking, took out a framed picture, from my kit bag, and put it on my bedside locker. Eddie took an interest and picked up my picture.

"PHWOOR! You lucky bastard, I'd give her one. That is what you call fit. Check it out boys."

I ignored the comments, and carried on laying out my sleeping bag, for the uncomfortable night ahead, sleeping on bedsprings.

"Got any nude pics of her new boy, eh, you're not married are you? Wocko asked."
"No, but she is…"

"You lucky bastard, so you're her toy boy, a bit on the side then?"
"... To my Dad!"

Eddie looked surprised, "That's your mum? If she was my old girl, I'd be crying home to mum tomorrow, how in god's name, did she manage to produce a piece of shit like you?"
"Were you breast fed as a child?" Wocko asked.

Everyone looked at him, there was silence, Wocko was embarrassed.

"What? Just curious, that's all!"

Suddenly Corpse entered the room.

"Watch out, Doctor Death's here again," came the comment from Eddie.
"That's it gents, it's time for beddie byes." Said Cpl Clark and proceeded to turn out the lights, much to my annoyance.

"Hold on with those lights, I haven't finished unpacking my kit yet." I said.
"You've had long enough Ward, see you all bright and early in the morning, and Eddie, no funny business."
"What me Corpse?"
"You know what I mean…. And it's Corporal."

I couldn't believe it, the door closed, now the room was in total darkness, apart from a ray of moonlight, shining on my mum's picture, which made me smile, it felt like my mum was still looking over me.

My kit was all over the place. Fuck it, I thought, it can wait till the morning. I decided to call it a day, and slipped into my **maggot,** to find I'd gotten a large bedspring sticking in my back, it was going to be a long night, little did I know how true that was.

"Ouch!!! Fucking great, I've got a fucking great spring sticking in my back."

"You can always top and tail with WOCKO, new boy," said Eddie
"Why do we have to have the lights out this early, it's only 11.30 pm?"
"It's a full moon, ain't it?
"What's that got to do with it?"
"Corpse wants to get into his coffin, before they drive a stake through his heart."

Everyone laughed and I carried on moaning.

"Eh new boy, can you turn your mum a little this way, so I can see her properly," Wocko said.
"Why do you want to see my mum?"

Then I heard his bed squeaking, surely not!

"Wocko you're disgusting, how could you do that over the kid's mother, you've only known her 10 minutes, you could have waited a few days at least," Eddie said.
I placed my mum's picture face down, "sorry mum."

"Sorry Wocko, but you need to see someone, how could you do that, that's my fucking mum, you bastard.
"If it had been your pet dog, he'd be doing the same, that's Wocko for you." Eddie replied.

I could believe it, I'd only been here 30 minutes, I'd been re-named, most of my fags had gone, I had a spring sticking up my arse, and my roommate was masturbating over my mum, great what's next?

"I wish I was back in training company...
I should've joined the artillery, like my dad told me to." I said feeling sorry for myself.

Big mistake, I shouldn't have said that, I soon realised I'd started my own artillery barrage, as boots and other heavy objects, were flung at me from all directions, then one boot hit me on the head.

"Ouch! That fucking hurt. Who threw that?" I shouted.

"Me," said Wocko.
"And it was meant to hurt, new boy, get some sleep, before you get my other size twelve."

It wasn't long before the loud snoring, farting, and occasionally someone talking in their sleep started, but I was used to that. I could just about make out the sound of the bugler, blowing the last post in the distance, which indicated it was midnight and the lights started to go out around the camp. It wasn't long before I was in the land of nod, after a long day. Maybe when I woke up this nightmare would be over.

Chapter Two

Despite the artillery barrage and bed spring, I slept ok, I thought! I woke up to the sound of a distant reveille, it was 0630hrs. And the smell of sheep shit. Sheep shit!!! I opened my eyes, I was surrounded by sheep. I was in the middle of a bloody field, the bastards, how did they do that!?

There was even a sheep lying on my bed. I quickly grabbed my sleeping bag, I was only wearing my **skiddies.** I headed back to the barrack room, half a mile away. I got back to find Doris, standing at the door waiting for me.

"What happened to you new boy, we thought you'd gone **AWOL**."
"Very funny, thanks a fucking bunch lad's."
"Stop moaning. Everyone gets something done to them on their first day, call it your initiation."

I stood in my empty bed space, looking confused and angry, wondering what to do next.

"A word of advice new boy, it pays to sleep with one eye open around here," Eddie said. "Just think yourself lucky, when Wocko had it done to him, he woke up under three feet of snow, and he lost a toe through frost bite, didn't you Wocko?" Doris piped up.
"That's right, and I've still got the toe to prove it."

I thought it was a wind up, until Wocko reached into his pocket, and pulled out his shrunken black toe, mounted on a key ring.

"Give over Wocko, you'll put me off my breakfast," Doris said turning away.

Suddenly the room was empty, apart from Eddie.

"Where is everyone going?" I asked.

"Breakfast."
"Could you give us a hand to get my bed back… please?"
"Sorry, can't miss breakfast, best meal of the day."
"But… but."

I had to get my bearings; I hurriedly put my uniform on and followed, I wasn't going to miss breakfast as well, I was starving. I finally made it to breakfast, just as they were pulling the shutters down.

"Sorry son, breakfast finished ten minutes ago. This isn't a bloody hotel you know," the cook said, looking at me as though I was something he'd trod in.
"You're joking, tell me you're joking."
"If you wanted breakfast, you should have got here on time."
"Ah, come on, there must be something left I can have. I'm starving."
"All I've got is beans."

"That'll do, I'd eat anything right now, pour em' on."

I held my plate out, but I wished I hadn't, when a massive dollop, of, burnt, stuck together, congealed beans, landed on it. I started to walk away, but I was stopped in my tracks, by a shout from the cook.

"Here don't forget your toast."

I hurried back, I needed something to soak the beans up with.

The cook, then stuck, 2 pieces of burnt, black toast, into the top of my pile of beans, now my meal resembled Mickey Mouse.

I decided to take the piss, but the cook didn't get my joke.

"I take it Keith Floyds been sacked then!!!"
"What?"
"Nothing."

"Enjoy!"
"Cheers!"

I grabbed a mug of lukewarm tea, and reluctantly joined my roommates. I sat down and stared at the banquet that lay before me.

"Look lads... look at the size of the helping of beans, new boy's got." Wocko said.

"Bloody favouritism that is, he must be shagging the cook," Doris replied.

I began playing with my food, debating whether to risk it and take a mouthful. No, I couldn't do it, I dropped my **diggers** onto the plate.

"I don't think I can stomach this, if this is breakfast, you can stick it up your arse."
"You'll get used to it, its food new boy, eat it, you need all the energy you can get!" Eddie said.
"Food, more like ball bearings, you mean."

"It's not the going in you want to worry about, it's when they come out. They're the army's new secret weapon. When you're down to your last bullet, jump out of your **trench**, point your arse at the enemy, and let them have it. Lethal at 100 yards, better than any grenade." Eddie replied laughing.
"There's only one place for this lot, and that's in the slop bin, for the pigs."

As I pushed my so called breakfast away, Wocko didn't waste any time, and grabbed my plate.

"Waste not, want not."

I sat back in amazement, as he started to shovel large mounds of beans, into his mouth.

"Your, eating habits are disgusting," Doris said grimacing.
"You're a walking skip WOCKO," said Eddie.

Wocko, offered me his left over cornflakes.

"Here, new boy, fair trade, get that down your neck, you've got to eat something."
"Cheers WOCKO, but no thanks."

Even though his intentions were all good, salad cream on corn flakes, didn't do anything for me. Eddie, was the first one to make a move, away from the table.

"We better get our skates on, or else Corpse will be after our blood, quite partial to a bit of the red stuff, old Dracula."

Wocko passed back to me, what was left of my beans, then they all got up and walked towards the exit.

"Why, what's the rush?"
"Room inspection in ten minutes," Eddie informed me, which made me nearly choke on my cup of tea.
"What? You've got to be joking."

Before I had even finished speaking, they were gone.

"Hold up, wait for me." I called out, as I headed for the door.

My roommates ignored my shouts, then I felt a presence behind me, I looked round, and Cookie was standing there, looking mean, he put his hand on my shoulder.

"You're not going anywhere pal, until you've eaten those beans, I made them special."
"But I'll be late."
"You wanted them, you eat them, oh and by the way, I got that joke, you were taking the piss weren't you, let's call it pay back... EAT!!!"

Chapter Three

The Razzer

I eventually escaped from the cook-house, and headed for my room. In the distance, I could see and hear Cpl Clark screaming at me, he was looking at his watch. I needed to get back quickly, and decided to take a short cut, over the parade square, big mistake.

"Get here you fucking cretin," I heard shouting coming from behind me, I turned round, "fuck," it was the Regimental Sergeant Major, the **Razzer,** a giant of a man, about 6 feet 6, he looked mad as hell, with veins popping out of his head. I u-turned and ran towards him, and stood to attention, then began my character assassination. In a voice loud enough to be heard for miles, he began to harangue me. "Only two people walk on this parade square, ME and GOD, and he only walks on it because I can't see him, or else I would Fucking **charge** him."

He started to make me laugh slightly, I knew it would anger him more, but I couldn't help it.

"What the fuck are you, laughing at, you fucking after birth, are you animal, vegetable or mineral, or the result of some sodomized, bastardized, relationship between all three? And what the fuck is that, dangling from your scrawny neck?"
"It's a crucifix, sir. My mum gave it to me."
"Why are you wearing jewellery, in uniform?"
"Cos' I'm a Christian, sir. Church of England."
"Well, I'm church of Egypt, but I don't wear a fucking Pyramid around my neck, do I? Get it off!!!!
"Yes Sir."
"Now fuck off, to where ever you were going, before I ram my pace stick through your ears, and ride you round camp, like a Kawasaki motorbike, with the speed of a thousand gazelles, move it."

He didn't have to tell me twice, I ran like hell towards my barrack room, I felt like I'd just had a lucky escape. I hope I never bump into him again, anytime soon. From one bollocking to another, now it was the Cpl Clarke's turn.

"Come on Ward, get a move on. You're late, I told you 0800 on parade."
"Sorry Corpse, err…. Corporal."
"You were late arriving here, late getting up, late for breakfast, if you don't sort yourself out, you'll be, "The late fucking private Ward," get in there and stand by your bed."
"But Corporal, I haven't got a bed."
"What do you mean, you haven't got a bed?"
"It's still in the field."

Cpl Clarke looked puzzled.

"What's it doing in the fucking field?"
"Shall I go and get it?"

Cpl Clark realised what had happened.

"Did Edwards have anything to do with this? Forget it, it's too late now, get inside."

I entered the room, they were all standing by their beds, laughing at me. I began tidying myself up, ready for the pending inspection, the childish giggling continued.

"Thanks lads. Thanks a bunch."
"Come on you lot, stop giggling like a bunch of school girls, and stand by your beds. They'll be here any second."
"But Corpse, I got to go." Eddie said, hopping from one foot to the other.
"Go where?"
"To the bog, I need to take a piss, you know I've got a weak bladder."
"You're not going anywhere Edwards; it's too late now, you'll have to hold it."

While Cpl Clark looked round the door, to see if they were coming to start the inspection, Eddie decided to relieve himself, behind his locker door. All we could hear, was the intermittent sound, of a filling water bottle.

"What the hell are you doing Eddie?" Wocko asked.
 "When you gotta go, you've gotta go!"

Eddie's timing was impeccable, as he stood back in front of his bed, seconds before they walked in. The only thing he forgot to put away was his **todger,** which he hurriedly managed to put away.

"Listen in. Room….atten…….tion!"

We all stood to attention, as the Platoon Commander and the Platoon Sergeant, entered the room.

The Platoon Commander, 2nd Lieutenant Robert Rupert Smith, Tall, good looking, mummy's boy, only just got through Officer training at Sandhurst. In my opinion, definitely too soft to be an officer, he thinks all his men should be wrapped in cotton wool, much to the Platoon Sergeant's distaste, very gullible, he also has a big problem, pronouncing his R's.

The Platoon Sergeant Bob Billings; nickname Beano, hates everything, typical drill Sergeant type, always spitting out his drill sergeant lingo, doesn't trust his men, his wife, even his dog, a first class arsehole. The Platoon Commander and the Platoon Sergeant couldn't be further apart.

 The first bed space they approached, was Eddie's. The Platoon Commander, began looking around Eddie's locker and bed space.

"What have you forgotten to do Soldier?"
"Err.... Feed the cat, sir?" Eddie answered him in a low voice.

I tried my hardest to keep a straight face.

"What did you say Edwards?" Sgt Billings asked.
"Nothing, sir."
"Have you seen the state of this man's miwah, Sgt Billings?"

Sgt Billings looked confused, due to the fact he had a big problem, interpreting what the platoon commander was saying.

"Beg your pardon, Sir... Miwah Sir?"
"Miwah."
"Oh mirror, sir... When was the last time you cleaned this mirror, Edwards?"

Eddie looked around at Sgt Billings.

"This morning, Sergeant."
"Bollocks! Face your front, and its Sir, there's an officer on parade. You didn't do a very good job, did you Edwards? Look at it."

Again, Eddie looked round at the Sergeant.

"I said face your front. It's in a shit state… I want it cleaned, straight after this inspection."
"Yes Sir. It'll be spotless Sir. You'll be able to see your face in it, Sir."

Wocko started to giggle.

"Shut up!!"

Sgt Billings leant forward, and had a word in Eddie's ear.

"Think you're a fucking comedian, don't you Edwards?"
"No Sergeant, I mean, no Sir."
"Well, I don't find you funny at all, remember Edwards, it's me who always has the last laugh, always."

He was lying of course, it was nearly always Eddie, who had the last laugh. There's an old saying in her majesty's forces, "You can't beat the system, its true apart from one exception… Eddie!!!

The Platoon Commander, then picked up Eddie's water bottle, and shook it.

"Water bottles are supposed to be empty for inspection. You know better than that soldier."
"What's in it, whisky again? You won't learn, will you Edwards?" Sgt Billings said, shaking his head.

Sgt Billings smiled, then proceeded to take out a hip flask, from his side pocket.

"I see you've come prepared, Sergeant. " The Platoon Commander said, smiling.

Thinking it was full of whisky, he opened the water bottle, and poured the contents straight into his hip flask, then smiled again, thinking he'd got one over on Eddie.

"I'm going to have to confiscate this, Edwards. Cpl Clark, put this man on weekend guard duties."

"Yes, Sergeant."

The PC then approached me, I stood in front of the space, where my bed should be.

"And who are you?"

I was just about to open my mouth, when Sgt Billings answered for me.

"Private Ward sir, joined us yesterday, fresh from Training Company."
"Settling in well Ward?"
"Yes."
"What wank am I, Pwivate?"
"Wank, Sir?"

There was more sniggering in the background, Wocko was busy having a Monty Python Biggus Dickus, trying not to laugh moment.

"Be quiet you lot," Sgt Billings shouted.

Then he started shouting down my ear, "Rank Ward, the platoon commander is a Lieutenant, that means you address Platoon Commander as sir, understood? You should know that by now, don't they teach them anything in training company."

"Yes Sir." I replied, still chuckling, it was hard not to, you just couldn't make it up.

"It's always nice to see a, fwesh face... err Sgt Billings, this man appears to have no bed, why is that?"

The PC looked at Sgt Billings, waiting for an answer. Sgt Billings looked at Cpl Clark, who looked dumbly at me.

"Well Cpl Clark, why hasn't this man got a bed?" Sgt Billings asked.

Cpl Clark didn't know what to say, and was lost for words.

"I... I haven't got a clue Sir, he had one last night, Sir, leave it with me, sir, I'll, get to the bottom of it."

"Wirly... so where did you sleep last night Ward?"
"In a field full of sheep, Sir."
"Sheep... What where you doing in a field full of sheep? No forget it, spare me the details, I don't want to know."

Eddie came to attention. "Permission to speak Sir. Private Ward was snoring loudly, so we removed him from the woom, Sir."

"You wemoved him from the woom?"
"That's wight, sir!"

Sgt Billings was by now, nearly blue in the face, trying his hardest not to laugh.

"Well, why didn't you just wake him up? The poor lad could have caught a chill... This isn't funny Sgt Billings, why are you laughing?"

"No Sir, it's not Sir."
"I will not have this Tom foolerwy, going on in my bawack wooms, is that clear?"
"Yes Sir... Point taken Sir."

The PC approached Private Day.

"Good turnout Day, as always."
"Thank you, Sir."
"Apart from the boots, I suggest you get Private Edwards, to show you how to bull boots pwoperly."

Sgt Billings pointed to Doris's shirt.

"And you have a button undone, Private Day."

It was one of Sgt Billing's pet hates, he raised his voice and addressed the room.

"That's how it starts gentlemen. It starts with an undone button, then it's an unfastened ammo pouch, before you know it, we're talking open submarine hatches. Do the fucker up now, Day!!!!"

The PC now approached Wocko; with caution, the smell hit him like a brick wall.

"Good god man! Watkinson you stink, and you look like a bag of shit, tied in the middle. Your bed isn't made pwoperly, and look at your locker man... Sgt Billings come and have a look at this."

They both peered into Wocko's, locker, all they could see was a giant black bin liner, full of festering clothes.

"Where is all your kit, Watkinson?"
"In the bag, Sir, that's my dirty washing for the laundrette, wash day is not until tomorrow sir."

The Sergeant and Platoon Commander, looked at each other in disbelief. Sgt Billings then peeled one of Wocko's socks off his locker door, with his pay stick and held it up.

"What the fuck is that, stuck to your locker door?"
"It's one of my socks Sir, I've been looking for that."

"It looks like it was trying to fucking escape."
"So that's what the smell is!" Wocko said.

The PC looked disgusted; Sgt Billings' nose, was now one millimetre away from Wocko's face.

"You are a fucking disgrace to the regiment soldier." Sgt Billings started to raise his voice. "I bet if I threw this sock out of the window, it would start eating the fucking grass? It's fucking alive, you are a walking fucking disease..."
  "Excuse me, Sergeant, but I really don't appreciate, you raising your voice around me. I find it most rude, and it hurts my feelings."

The Platoon Sergeant and PC just stand there, opened mouthed, gob smacked! Sgt Billings was the first to react.

"Show Parade tonight." He shouted.

Show parade, was a pain in the arse for any **squaddie,** instead of dossing on your bed all night, or getting pissed down the Naafi, it meant you had to turn up at the guardroom, at 6 pm in combat dress, then do fatigues for the next 2 hours. Then at 10pm you had to report to the guardroom again, in full number 2 dress, to be inspected by the duty officer, and if your turnout wasn't good enough, he'd make you come back every hour of the night, until it was. Wocko was used to Show parade, he'd done that many of them, he could write a book about it, it was supposed to be a punishment, it didn't work for Wocko.

Wocko smiled "I'm already on Show Parade tonight, Sir."

Sgt Billings stopped in his tracks.

"Okay, tomorrow night, then, smart arse."
"And tomorrow night, Sir. In fact, I'm fully booked up for the rest of the week. I could look in my diary and see when I'm next available Sir!"

Sgt Billings realised he was getting nowhere.

"Shut up Watkinson. I give up, I'm a beaten man, all I know is, if we ever go to war, just make sure you're next to me, the enemy would run a fucking mile, if they smelt you coming. You can join Edwards, on guard duty this weekend."

The Platoon commander, finished his room inspection and turned to Sgt Billings.

"Bwief the men, Sergeant. I'll see you this evening, cawie on."

Sgt Billings saluted and the PC wandered off.

"Listen in room, room atten......tion... Stand at ease. Stand easy, well... well... well... you lot never fail to amaze me.

"When I was a young lad, I left my plastic soldiers in front of the fire and they melted, when I was crying my mother said, "Don't worry son, you'll have REAL soldiers, of your very own one day, to play with." - YOU LOT HAVE MADE MY MOTHER INTO A FUCKING LIAR!!!!! You are all confined to camp this weekend. This room is a disgrace, it's bogging. Some of you lot want taking out onto the Parade Square and pulling through, hosing down, or even better shot. The good news is, the Platoon Commander, has given you the rest of the day off..."

The whole room cheered, but that didn't last long, there must be a reason why we'd be given the day off.

"So you can prepare yourself for tonight's Navigation Exercise... Carry on Cpl Clark."
"Right you heard the Platoon Sergeant. Make sure your kit's ready, for tonight's Night Nav, before you all start wandering off."

Corpse left the room, and everyone jumped back on their bed, apart from me of course.

"That Sgt Billings is a bit of a bastard, isn't he?" I said.
"Who BEANO, he's ok, he just gets a little excited every now and then," Eddie said.

"BEANO... Why do you call him BEANO?"
Eddie chuckled "all he ever says is
There will **BE NO leave.**
There will **BE NO time off.**
There will **BE NO sport. .**"

Eddie didn't waste any time, he knew where he wanted to go.

"Right, who's coming down the NAAFI, for a game of pool? What about you, new boy?"
"You heard Cpl Clark. We're supposed to be preparing for tonight's Night Nav."
"Prepare what? Bollocks to that. Just chuck your kit on, put your mind in neutral, and follow the twat in front of you. We usually get lost anyway. Corpse couldn't read a map if it was tattooed to his fucking eye lids. Well, come on somebody, give me a game. I've got a big match coming up. I need to practice; come on, what about you Doris... Wocko?"

Still pissed off from earlier, Doris took his boots out, and started bulling them.

"Sorry I'm busy"
"Wocko mate, come on."

Wocko was looking through his bag of washing, then started to empty the large black bag out on his bed, and the floor, it began to stink the room out. We couldn't get out of the room fast enough.

"I've changed my mind, I will have that game of pool after all," I said.
"Wait for me too." Doris said.

Chapter Four

THE BRIEFING

We travelled to the training area, by Bedford 4 ton truck. The journey would take around an hour, I couldn't believe it, we'd only been travelling 10 minutes and most people were asleep. I'd drawn the short straw and sat next to Wocko, luckily the draught coming through the canopy, fanned away his smell.

He then spent most of the journey, asking me if I had any more pictures of my mum, I didn't want. He told me he'd to buy them off me, then he started trying to persuade me, it would be a good idea, for us both to go on leave together, so I could introduce him to my mum!

We arrived at the start point, climbed off the Bedford 4 Tonner, then the next minute we were all crammed into a tent, ready for the

PC's briefing, or should I say bweefing, on the night navigation exercise.

We were sat in our section, all the men were dressed in full camouflage uniform, then the **cam cream** (face paint,) got passed around. We all had our own way of applying it, there was always some idiot, who'd start messing around, the next minute I had a finger full of this stuff in my ear. Before I got the chance to retaliate, the briefing was underway. I started to take notes, the heading on the blackboard, '**EXERCISE DEAD STUDENT'.**

"Okay, I'll go through the main points again. You'll move from here to the start point, for a spot inspection, which you'll be scored on. Then each Section Commander, will be given eight gwid weferences. You'll move out in ten minute intervals. For evewy check point you reach, you'll weceive two points. And don't forget, wemain on your guard at all times. Sgt Billings and I will be acting as the enemy, if we catch you, you'll lose one point, and be taken back in the Land Wover two miles. So, don't forget, stay alert. Did you hear that Edwards?"

Eddie was asleep and suddenly woke up, when Wocko poked him in the ribs.

"What... Eh... yes, Sir"
"What did I say then?" The PC asked.
"Don't forget to wear a skirt, at all times."
"Platoon Sgt, deduct one point from Pwivate Edwards's Section. Wight, move out evweyone."

Cpl Clark turned to Eddie, and gave him a dirty look.

"What're you looking at me like that for?"
"We haven't even gone anywhere, and we've lost a point already." Said Cpl Clark.

Sgt Billings grabbed everyone's attention "Right Section Commanders, get your men outside, ready for inspection."

We all moved outside and lined up, ready for inspection, it was starting to get cold, icy cold and snowing I was definitely not looking forward to this. Corporal Clark was busy plotting the check points onto his map, while Sgt Billings started to inspect us all, I was the first person he came to.

"Get more cam cream on Ward, I can still see your ugly face."
"But Sgt, it gives me blackheads." Not the wisest thing, I'd ever said.
"Does it really? And I suppose your y fronts, give you nappy rash."
"Stop talking shite, didn't they teach you anything in training? Why do we put cam cream on Ward?"
"Err... to break up the outline of your face, so you blend into the background."
"Correct, Fucking hell you did take something in, in training."

Sgt Billings pushed the tube of cream hard into my chest.

"Get more cam cream on, before I break up the outline of your face, then you'll definitely blend into the background."

He next approached Eddie, it was quite obvious he'd put too much on. Sgt Billings just stood and stared at him, shaking his head, he then approached Pte Day, his face was caked in it as well, you, could only see the whites of their eyes.

"Are you two fucking brothers?" Sgt Billings asked.

Doris and Eddie looked at each other, with a dumb look on their faces. Sgt Billings then walked up to Wocko, the Sergeant looked surprised.

"Well done Private Watkinson, that's how you put cam cream on. Nice and evenly all over, everyone else take note."
"But Sergeant, I haven't put any on yet."

Sgt Billings, expression spoke for its self.

"Right gentlemen; let's have you jumping up and down. Remember, you're patrolling at night, that means no banging or clanging. I don't want to hear a sound... Well, what are you waiting for, jump come on, 'I've got all night, I'm not bothered, I've got a salad in the fridge and my wife is ugly'."
"JUMP you fucking' cretins, my sister can jump higher than you waste of rations, and she is in a wheel chair."

We all started jumping, then we heard the most almighty clatter of mess tins etc, also a strange sloshing sound. Sgt Billings didn't look happy.

"Stop!!!! You lot are un-fucking believable, the enemy would hear you lot coming from ten miles away, it sounds like a skeleton wanking in a biscuit tin. This is a night exercise, gents, all of you get your kit off and sort it out. Not you Edwards, come here"

Eddie stood in front of him, with a puzzled look on his face.

"What is it Sgt Billings?"
"Jump up and down."
The sound of liquid sloshing around, could be clearly heard by everyone.

"What the hell is that? "
"I can't hear a thing Sergeant."
"Really, you sound like a washing machine on heat, open your jacket."

Eddie opened his Jacket and out dropped a hot water bottle.

"Oh shit, how did that get in there?" Eddie said.
"You tell me Edwards, a hot water bottle, you fucking fairy. I'll be having words with you later, get back in line with the others, oh and by the way that's another point deducted."
"Listen in. Out of a maximum of five points, I'm awarding you a grand total of one point, and that was for Watkinson's face camouflage… And that was a fluke. So gents, you've got a lot of catching up to do already, let's hope you have a better Night Nav. Cpl Clark you can move out now. Do you know where you're going?"
"Yes, Sergeant, I've got it all sorted."

We all lined up in single file, behind each other, it was going to be a long night. Stick with me Wardie, Eddie said and you'll be alright, I wasn't convinced.

Cpl Clark started to move off, still busy trying to make sense of his map. We all followed him, like a flock of sheep, down the road, when we heard a shout from Sgt Billings.

"Cpl Clark."

We all stopped in our tracks, bumping into each other, Cpl Clark looked back at Sgt Billings, who was pointing the other way.

"It's that way."
"Course it is," said Cpl Clark.
"You lot are about as good as a one legged man, in an arse kicking competition!!!!!!"

The section did a U turn, and we all started to pass Sgt Billings, one by one, Eddie made a comment.

"Beautiful night for it Sergeant."
"What are you, a fucking weather man now?" Replied Sgt Billings.
"God help us, we're all going to die, pray for us Sarge!!"
"Cheer up. You're getting paid for this!!"

We all started making sheep bleating sounds, as we passed Sgt Billings and disappeared into the darkness. It was then I realised, we were doomed.

Chapter Five

Lost

What seemed like ages later, we were all moving across an open field, in single file, we all had our heads up our arses, we'd lost interest miles back, there was a lot of moaning, it was very dark and cold, and we were lost.

"We've been going two hours, and we haven't even reached our first checkpoint yet," said Eddie, and then it was Doris's turn to moan. "Admit it Clarky, we're lost aren't we?

We seemed to be going round in circles, all we wanted to do was get back in the warm and we all wished this pointless exercise was over.

Then suddenly, Cpl Clark stopped in his tracks, we all stopped and crashed into each other behind him, it wasn't the first time.

"What's this road doing here? Said Cpl Clark this isn't right. There shouldn't be a road here."

Eddie reassured him... sort of.

"You're right Corpse... it's the map that's wrong, you always seem to get a bad one."
"Shut it you, it's not my fault. How can I see any road markings in this snow?"

He was right, it was a complete white out.
 We were all now in a small circle, looking at the map, the torch started to fade, and we had no spare batteries, morale was low.
I decided it was time I tried to rescue the situation.

 "Let me have a look at the map, I'll tell you where we are." Eddie soon put me in my place.
"Button it new boy, Corpse knows where he's going, don't you Corpse?"

All of a sudden Cpl Clark handed me the torch, I couldn't believe it, they, were actually going to listen to me.

"Here, make yourself useful. Hold that and point it at the map."

I know I was only holding the torch, but it was a start and I could now see the map.

"Now, according to this map we're here, the checkpoint is there, so, we are faced with one choice, do we go left or right?"

There was a moment's pause while nobody spoke until Eddie opened his mouth.

"You're like a lighthouse in the desert Clarky, bright, but fucking useless."

Cpl Clark had, had enough of Eddie's piss taking, and faced up to him. The pressure was showing, as they started to tussle with each other.

"Listen Edwards, I ain't taking any more of your shit, If, I wanted to hear an arsehole, I would have farted."

Then I made my move, if I was going to rescue the situation, it was now or never. I stepped between them both, like a referee in a boxing match.

"Well, it's got to be left hasn't it?" I said.
"Who asked you?" Doris said.
"The check point's near Titmarch, isn't it?"
"Err… yes!" Cpl Clark acknowledged.

I then shone the torch at the sign post, which was right in front of us.

"What does it say on that sign up there?"

The sign read, Titmarsh 2 miles. Wocko patted me on the back.

"He's right, you know, Wardie, I love you, and I want to have your babies."
"Get away from me, you nonce."
"Steady on Wocko, I wouldn't go that far, nice one, Wardie." Said Eddie.
"Oh, now I'm Wardie, am I?"
"The kid's a genius." Said Doris"
"Shush," said Eddie, "can you hear that?"

Suddenly we heard the sound of a wagon.

"Quick, everyone, get down." Corpse said.
"Hit the deck, it's them."

We all crouched behind a mound of snow, at the side of the road, my hero status didn't last long.

"You twat, new boy, you've given our position away, shining that torch." Whispered Eddie.

The wagon stopped, about twenty yards away, and the Platoon Commander and Sgt Billings jumped out.

"Right you lot, let's have you. You're captured. Come on, stand up, I know you're there," said Sgt Billings.

Wocko started to stand up, but was soon pulled back down again by Eddie.

"Get down you idiot," whispered Eddie.
"Are you sure you saw something Sgt Billings?" Said the PC.
"Yes Sir, they are definitely here, I'm sure of it. I saw a torch light."

Suddenly I got a nudge in the ribs from Eddie.

"You see, I told you. If we get caught, your dead meat, new boy." I wondered why Eddie was so upset, and where did his don't give a shit attitude go!

Then someone let rip and farted.
SHHHHHHUSH.
Sgt Billings sniffed the air.

"I'd know that smell anywhere, that's Watkinson's smell. Come on, stand up, I know you're there... This isn't doing any of us any good. Come and have a lift in my nice warm wagon."

Sergeant Billings only had to walk a few yards, and we'd be discovered, I guess he didn't want to get his boots wet in the snow. The platoon commander climbed back into the wagon he'd had enough.

"Let's go, Sgt Billings. There's no one here, apart from us, and a few sheep."
"Just give it another five minutes Sir."

Sgt Billings then raised his voice.

"I'll tell you what, why don't you get out those fish 'n' chips Sir."

It was obviously a ploy and Wocko fell for it.

"Fish and chips did he say fish and chips, that's it, I can't stand this anymore."

Wocko tried to get up and surrender. The temptation of fish and chips, was too great for him. But Eddie held him back, and put his hand over his mouth.

"Get down you idiot, it's a trap."
"Fish and chips, Sgt Billings!? What are you talking about?"
Sgt Billings walked back in the wagon and climbed in.

"Forget it Sir, let's go."

They drove away. Everyone started to get up.

"Get down you fools. " Said Cpl Clark, "we're staying put for a while, until they're well out of sight, they could double back."

Meanwhile, in the wagon, Sgt Billings took out his hip flask, and started to unscrew the top.

"I'm telling you, Sir, they were there alright."
"So what if they were, and we had taken them two miles back. They're not even at the first check point yet, camp's only two miles away, what would be the point in that."

Sgt Billings offered the PC a drink.

"Here, have a swig of this Sir, that'll put hairs on your chest, courtesy of Private Edwards."
"No thanks, but you go ahead, I'm driving."

Sgt Billings took a swig.

"This weather's getting worse Sergeant."

Sgt Billings suddenly spewed out the contents of his mouth, all over the dashboard.

"What's up, too strong for you Sergeant?"
"I'll kill him."
"Kill who? That must be stwong stuff."

Back in the field, Eddie had fallen asleep and was snoring loudly. I was trying my hardest to keep warm sat behind him, the last man. The moon had disappeared behind the clouds, it was now pitch dark.

"Eddie, Eddie, wake up. Ask them when we are moving out, it should be safe by now. We've been sitting here for 20 minutes, for fuck's sake."

It soon became obvious, Eddie and I were the only 2 in the field, we'd, been left behind.

"There's nobody there, they've gone." He said.
"I knew something was amiss, due to the lack of Wocko's trade mark smell, it had gone. I don't believe it… you fell asleep didn't you." I said.
"No, I didn't," said Eddie.
"Yes, you did, you were snoring that loud you woke me up!"
"Aha, so you were **gonking** as well then?" Eddie replied.

I wasn't happy, lost, on my first exercise.

"Now what are we going to do? It's freezing.... No map, torch or compass and its pitch dark."
"Well, you know what they say, if you're lost, head for the nearest signs of life." Eddie said

Just as he said that, the moon, decided to make another appearance. I got to my feet and looked around, all I could see was snow and more snow, lit up by a near full moon.

"Signs of life? The only signs of life around here, are a few fucking' sheep, and I can't see them giving us a piggy back ride back to camp."
"It just so happens, there's a pub, just over that hill."

Eddie then pointed to a flickering light in the distance.

"Of course, there is Eddie, and look disco lights and a strip joint, oh and a casino. Or it could even be, the star of fucking David, come on, let's get back on our camels and follow it."

"You're not funny new boy, you need to calm down a bit," Eddie stood looking dumbly at me.
"Where!? Oh, I see it now, It, must be Las Vegas."
"You've come out your shell new boy, I'm telling you, just over that hill, there's a pub, trust your uncle Eddie"
"Are you taking the piss, forget it, I'm staying put till they find me."
"Suit yourself, I'm off." Said Eddie.

I couldn't believe it, Eddie just strolled off into the distance. I had no choice but to follow him reluctantly, staying together was always the safe policy, buddy, buddy system and all that bollocks.

"Hold on, wait for me, you better be right Eddie."
"Trust me, I can smell beer from ten miles away."

Cpl Clark, and what was left of his section, arrived at the first check point, his lads were tired out. The PC and Sgt Billings were standing there waiting. The moon had now disappeared behind the clouds again, it was now snowing heavily.

"I don't believe it, it's Robin Hood and his Merry Men. They've actually made it to a checkpoint." Said Sgt Billings.
"Where's those fish and chips Sarge." Said Wocko.

Sgt Billings turned to the PC.

"You see Sir, I told you they were there... and there's that smell again."

"Okay, okay, Sgt Billings, you were wight, I was wong. It doesn't matter now does it? Tell them the good news Sergeant"

"Gather round you lot," said Sgt Billings, "I've got some good news for you chaps. Due to the adverse weather conditions, the Exercise Dead Student is now cancelled. So get your kit off, grab a brew, then get on the wagon. We move out in 20 minutes."

Everybody cheered, apart from me and Eddie, because we were not fucking there. We were in the middle of nowhere, freezing our nuts off.

Chapter Six

The Pub

After walking for what seemed like miles, the flickering light in the distance became a reality, and it wasn't long before we came across, what looked like a country pub!

"I don't believe it, you were right, it's a bloody pub, how, the fuck did you know that?"

Eddie looked back at me and smiled.

"Don't ask, it's a built in sense, you either have the gift or you don't. Come on, let's get in the warm, I'm gagging for a pint."

We walked in. It was a country pub alright, the heat from the glowing fire hit me straight away, there was a low ceiling, the, place was full of locals. Eddie approached the bar.

"I expected you an hour ago, where've you been luvvy?" Said the barmaid.

I looked at Eddie, suspiciously, I could smell a rat.

"Long story, said Eddie… two large ones, please Katie, darling."
"Err… is he old enough?"
"Of course I'm old enough," I said feeling insulted.
"Aren't you going to introduce me then Eddie?"
"Oh yeah, Wardie, this is Katie. Wardie has just joined us, fresh from Training Company."
"So he's a virgin is he? Sounds interesting, so are you breaking him in, or do you want me to do it?"

I felt slightly embarrassed, she was old enough to be my mum, for fuck's sake, shit she started winking at me. Katie finished pulling the pints.

"There you go boys."

"Have one yourself Katie." Said Eddie, as he handed over a 10 pound note.

Katie turned towards the till.

"You planned this, didn't you?"
"What, you and Katie you mean?"
"Don't mess about Eddie, you tampered with Corpse's grid references, didn't you, I'm not stupid."
"I haven't got the faintest idea what you're talking about, here drink your beer."

I put my pint down on the bar

"You know damn well, what I'm talking about."

Eddie turned to me and looked surprised.

"I hope you're not accusing me of sabotage, disobeying orders, and putting men's lives at risk, just for a few poxy pints of lager?"
"Yes."

Eddie passed me my beer.

"Okay, you're right... and for your information, I didn't tamper with Corpse's grid references, I didn't have to, I knew we were doomed from the start. I know this area like the back of my hand, due to the many nights I've staggered back to camp. So if I could do that pissed, getting here was easy, now here, get that down your neck and shut the fuck up, what's done is done."
"We'll get a court martial for this."
"No, we won't, calm down will you, everything's under control, it's freezing cold outside. So we stay here until closing time, then we jump in a taxi back to camp, and tell them we successfully navigated ourselves, all the way home, without a map or compass. We'll get a bloody medal you'll see."

I shook my head in disbelief. Eddie downed his pint.

"No, I don't think so." I said.

"Put another one in here Katie, pet... anyway I've got a pool match in two minutes."
"You what?"
"It's the final; I'm playing the pub's unbeaten champion. There he is in the corner."

I looked over and I saw a giant of a man, built like a brick shit house, he was taking a practice shot. He cleared most of the balls on the table with just one shot, and then looked up at Eddie and smiled.

"Him... I said, you've got no chance."
"It's not a wrestling match, it's a pool match. I bet you the taxi fare home, I beat him."

Eddie waved at Granville, that was the giant's name.

"Be with you in a minute Granville."

Eddie passed me his empty glass." Your round new boy."

Meanwhile, back at the first check point, Cpl Clark was busy checking his men, as they loaded their kit onto the wagon.

"Eh, where's, Wardie and Eddie?"
"Don't ask me, I thought they were up front." Replied Doris, while loading his kit onto the wagon.
"No, they were behind you."
"The only person behind me was Wocko. I know that for a fact. I could smell him."
 "Piss off Doris." Said Wocko.

Cpl Clark began to look worried.

"Come on guys give me a break, this is serious, where are they?"

Cpl Clarke didn't realise the PC was standing right behind him.

"What's sewious Cpl Clark?" Said the PC.
"Well, it could be, Sir, we're two men short."
"What! Are you sure?"

"Yes Sir"
"Who?"
"Privates Ward and Edwards, Sir."
"Gweat, that's all we need."
"Sorry Sir."

The PC began to panic, as he realised the implications of losing two men on exercise. "Sowee, sowee, that's not good enough. I'll have your stwipes for this Cpl Clark. Do you wealise they could die out there."

Sgt Billings tried to calm the situation down.

"I doubt it Sir, they're probably in a pub somewhere, knowing Edwards."
"This is a sewious situation."
"Yes Sir, you're right Sir... right, you lot, get your kit on, I want them men found. Cpl Clark, get your men in the other wagon, and get searching, and keep to the roads, we don't want anybody else lost. We'll meet back here in one hour."

Back in the Pub, the match was well under way, Granville missed a shot. Eddie was winning. I was cheering Eddie on, but stopped when Granville gave me a look, as though he was about to rip my head off.

"Come on Eddie, come on, you can do it, come on."

By that time, I was starting to feel a little pissed. I was on my 4th pint and Katie was starting to look younger. She wandered over and put her arm round me. That was it, I was in love.

Eddie won the match, by potting the black with a fluky shot. Granville got up to shake his hand angrily. Eddie screamed in pain.

"Next time sonny, next time."
"You've won, well done." I shouted.

Eddie gritted his teeth, as he turned away from Granville. He looked like he was in some pain.

What's up Eddie?" I asked.

"It's me wrist, I think he's busted it shaking my hand."
"There goes your love life." Said Katie.
"It's not bloody funny."
"Don't worry about it. I'll get you a whisky, that'll take the pain away." Katie said.

We were standing at the bar facing the entrance, when suddenly the PC walked in. The room went quiet. Me and Eddie clocked him in time and ducked, then crawled behind the bar out of sight.

"Yes sir, what can I do for you, a pint is it?" Said Katie giggling.
"No thanks…. Err…. We've been conducting an exercise, out on the training area and we seem to have lost two of our chaps."

"Oh dear, on a night like this tut, tut; it's freezing out there. I hope they're ok, those poor devils"

"Yes, they seem to have strayed from their Section."

The PC's eyes began wandering around the room, getting strange looks back from the locals.

"What do they look like sir? Don't tell me all in green, black boots, carrying weapons and they've got dirty faces."

The PC smiled in anticipation, hoping she knew where they were.

"Yes, that's them have you seen them."
"No, we haven't seen anything like that around here, have we lads?"

The PC then addressed the room full of locals.

"Have any of you seen a couple of my lads?"

The locals shook their heads with a serious look on their faces, there was an uneasy silence.

"Well, if you do, could you wing the camp stwaight away, this is the number."

The PC wrote the contact number on his note pad, then ripped it out of his notebook, and handed it over to Katie.

Katie took the note. "Of course we will, now are you sure you don't want a quick one."
"I beg your pardon?"

Katie held up an empty pint glass.

"A dwink".
"Err... no thanks, I've got to go. I must find those lads, before the weather gets any worse, good night to you."

"Good night to you, and good luck."

The PC walked out, the door shut behind him. A few seconds passed, then the PC re-entered the pub quickly, hoping to catch us coming out from our hiding place, but we didn't. Everyone stared at the PC, who looked a little embarrassed. To try and hide his embarrassment, he walked up to the bar
"Err…. A bag of cwisp please."
"What flavour?"
"Err cheese and onion please."

Katie reached down and I passed her the crisps. Eddie was on his back, a cider barrel tap was in full flow, straight into Eddie's mouth. I reached over and turned it off.

"There you go, 30 pence, please."

The PC gave her the money, left the Pub and climbed into the wagon, Sgt Billings was sitting in the driving seat with the engine running.

"Well?"
"They're not in there, Sgt Billings." .
"I bet they are, let me go in there, let's search the place."
"Sgt Billings, you can't just barge in there and search the place. I'm telling you they're not in there, okay?"
"Sorry Sir, you're right. Where to next"
"Oh, just dwive on, let's find Cpl Clark and see if he's had better luck."
"Right you are, sir."
"Oh blow it; I will have some of that whisky now, Sgt Billings."

Sgt Billings looked at him wide eyed, as the PC grabbed the flask from the dashboard. Sgt Billing's panicked, knowing his Platoon Commander was about to sample Eddie's matured, rancid, piss.

"Sir, you can't drink that, it's……"
"Why ever not, you did, it can't be that bad, like you said earlier, it's just what one needs, on a night like this?"

"You just can't. It'll be too strong for you, Sir."
"Wubbish, it's just what I need to calm my nerves. If I lose these two soldiers, my neck's on the line and yours. Exercise Dead student will be a reality."

The PC took a long swig. Sgt Billings sat tense waiting for the explosion, he was sure would follow.
"Phew…choke…" The PC's voice weakened "this is stwong stuff, just what the doctor ordered."

He then amazingly took another gulp, he liked it. Sgt Billings sat staring out the window, **gobsmacked.**

"Do you want this last dwop Sergeant?"
"No Sir, I'll let you finish it off sir."
"Are you sure?"
"Go ahead Sir… I'm driving"
"Good man, I'll have to have words with young Edwards, and find out where gets his whisky from."

They drove on up the road.

Eddie and I slowly rose from behind the bar, by now we were both very drunk.

"Phew…. For a minute there, I thought you were going to drop us in it, Katie," said Eddie. "Two more beers lads?"
"No, make it two double whiskies. I'll buy, " said Eddie.
"Come on Eddie, it's about time we got a taxi and headed back to camp. Listening to the PC, it sounds like the whole Battalion is out looking for us now."

Eddie didn't seem to care. "You worry too much Wardie," then Katie broke the bad news. "You won't get a taxi now, boys, they won't come all the way out here. The weather's too bad."
"That's great." I said

"It looks like we're walking, don't worry, Eddie's got it all under control. Here, have another drink!"

Katie was now getting really fresh with me, and made her move, suddenly she was all over me and I was starting to enjoy it.

"You can always stop here tonight."

I whispered in Eddie's ear.
"Eh Eddie, I reckon I'm in here mate, she's all over me."
Eddie whispered back.

"I don't think so son."
"I'm telling you I've scored and I'm not bothered, she's twice my age, "hic," you're just jealous... shall we stay the night or what?"

Just then, Katie forcefully shoved her tongue down my throat, and her hands were all over me, I was, loving it!

"You better ask her husband," said Eddie.
"Husband?"
"He's over there."

I looked over and Granville was looking at me. He looked mad as hell. I let go of Katie, my thoughts of a night of passion now quelled.

Chapter Seven

Time to go

"Come on Eddie, it's time to go, sorry Katie another time perhaps."
"That might be a good idea right now," said Eddie.

Eddie poured what was left of his whiskey, in his hip flask.

Corporal Clark's wagon, had stopped at a junction. Cpl Clark was looking at his map. Doris was driving.

"This road shouldn't be here."
"I don't believe it, are you telling me we're lost again," Doris said.
"You didn't by any chance work for the council before you joined up, did you Corpse?" Wocko shouted, from the back of the vehicle.

"No, but he's going to start his own taxi firm when he gets out, aren't you Corpse?" Doris responded.
"Take a right here, no, on second thoughts, make it a left, no right."
"Make your fucking mind up, are you sure?"
"I'm telling you, it's left."
"Well, this river is telling me it's not." Said Doris
"It's alright Doris, wagon's float, don't they Corpse?"
"Another word out of you, and you'll be in that bloody river."
"Sorry I spoke."
"That'll be the first wash, you've had for a while, Wocko," said Doris.
"Turn round and go back the way you came."

Sheep bleating sounds are coming from the back of the wagon, as they drove into the distance.

We both managed to get out of the pub unharmed, we walked down the road, pissed as farts, singing, arms round each other. Eddie had got his arm in a makeshift sling Katie had made him, suddenly our singing stopped.

"Hold on, do you know where we're going?" I asked.
"No!"
"Where's Cpl Clark, when you need him, Eddie?"

We both laughed that much, we fell over, then, I started to be sick. We stuck out like a sore thumb, on a hill silhouetted.

In the distance we could see two wagons, coming from opposite directions, heading towards each other. The two sets of headlights met, Eddie and I were bang in the middle, looking like scared rabbits. Cpl Clark got out of one wagon, the PC and Sgt Billings the other, all of them walked toward us.

"It looks like the games up Wardie, bloody hell they look mad. Don't say a word, leave the explaining to me," said Eddie.

It was the last thing on my mind at that moment. I was still decorating the road with vomit. The PC looked down at us, like an angry father.

"Where the hell have you two been? We've been searching for you, all bloody night."

Eddie managed to stand up and started his defence. Sgt Billings looked on with his arms folded.

"This better be good Edwards."

Eddie cleared his throat, and what came out of his mouth next, was pure fiction.

"Well... err.... We got sort of lost.... Err..... I slipped in the snow you see, and sprained my ankle. I mean my wrist, and by the time I could inform Cpl Clark, he was too far ahead. If it wasn't for Private Ward here, staying with me and administering first aid and taking me to safety, I'd have probably frozen to death. I was suffering from shock at the time you see."

The PC and Sgt Billings looked at each other.

"Well, it sounds feasible to me Sgt Billings"
"Bull shit… I'm sorry Sir, but I don't believe that for one second, he's talking 100% bollocks, I can smell alcohol. You smell like a brewery. You've been in the pub, haven't you?"
 "Impossible Sgt Billings, I checked the pub wemember."
"So why do they smell of booze then, Sir, and Ward looks drunk to me."
"Permission to speak Sir." Said Eddie
"… After saving my life Sir, Private Ward……"
 "I'm going to fucking cry in a minute, you're breaking my fucking heart Edwards," said Sgt Billings.

"Will you be quiet Sergeant, let the man speak." Said the PC.
"As I was saying, after saving my life, I suddenly realised Ward himself was going down with exposure. All I could do Sir, was to give him a drink, from my hip flask, to warm him up."

Eddie pulled out a large hip flask, from inside his jacket. The PC grabbed the flask and sniffed it. Sgt Billings couldn't believe the PC was taking it all in.

"Likely story."
"Sgt Billings, can't you see what these men have been through. Look at his wist for cwying out loud, and Ward is showing all the signs of someone suffering from exposure, someone get this man a blanket."
"Cpl Clark, get these men in the sick bay and give yourself a pat on the back, you've got some fine men here."

We clumsily climbed into the back of the wagon with Wocko's help. Sgt Billings and the PC were walking towards their vehicle.

"Well, did you win?" Wocko asked.
"Yeah, he was easy," Eddie replied.
"Nice one."

As we drove away, we could hear Sgt Billings and the PC talking.

"Sir, they're lying."
"Sgt Billings, why do you continually disagwee with me?"
"I don't Sir."
"Yes, you do, you should never disagwee with me, especially in front of the men."
"I don't."
"You do Sgt Billings."

We both spent the night in sick bay, the following morning, Eddie had his arm strapped up and I was feeling rough from the night before.

"What happened last night, my head's throbbing."
"You're a hero Wardie, you saved my life, remember?"

Then I began to remember everything and started to panic.

"Oh my god, it's all coming back to me now, we're in the shit, aren't we?"
"Stop flapping, it's all under control. We're on easy street. Stick to our story and we'll be alright, they might even give us a medal for what we've been through."

Sgt Billings entered the room and surprisingly looked in a good mood. He had his hands behind his back, he was hiding something.

"Hello Sarge."
"Hello boys, how are you feeling after your little ordeal? The Platoon Commander asked

me to pop in and see if you were alright, and to see if you needed anything."
"I'm a lot better, thanks Sarge."
"And you Eddie, how's your wrist?"
"I'll live Sarge, I might have to have a few weeks off, but I'll live... Oh Sarge, are you hiding something? You haven't, you've bought us a present, haven't you. What is it? Grapes, a box of chocolates, a bottle of whisky perhaps."
"No, it's something you forgot to pick up last night. Someone kindly left it at the guard room."

Our faces dropped, when a smiling Sgt Billings, presented Eddie with his pool trophy.

"I think you've both got some explaining to do."

So there we were, wearing green overalls, one behind the other, being marched in double quick time, by Sgt Billings, straight to the guard room and then into the cells.

We later, both received 14 days.

END

I hope you enjoyed my story and it brought back a few memories.

In Army Barmy 2, "lost in the Jungle." The battalion is posted to Belize, Central America, will they all survive!?

Glossary

AWOL/Absent without leave
Barrack room/Accommodation
Bed space/ The area around your bed
Bulling Boots/Polishing boots to a high sheen like glass
Cam cream/Camouflage cream
Charge/On report
Cook House/Canteen
Cpl/Corporal
Diggers/Knife Fork and Spoon
Gob smacked/Surprised
Gonking/sleeping
Locker/Wardrobe
Maggot/Sleeping bag
Naafi/Navy, Army, Air Force Institute Shop
Non Tac/Non tactical
PC/Platoon Commander
Razzer/Regimental Sergeant Major/RSM
Room jobs/Cleaning duties
Sgt/Sergeant
Skiddies/Underpants
Squaddie/A soldier
Square/The parade square

Todger/Penis
Trench/Hole in the ground
UXB/Unexploded Bomb
Wagon/Military vehicle
Wank mag/Pornographic magazine

Printed in Great Britain
by Amazon